El Salvador
the land

Greg Nickles

A Bobbie Kalman Book

The Lands, Peoples, and Cultures Series

Crabtree Publishing Company
www.crabtreebooks.com

The Lands, Peoples, and Cultures Series

Created by Bobbie Kalman

Coordinating editor
Ellen Rodger

Assistant editor
P.A. Finlay

Production coordinator
Rosie Gowsell

Project development, photo research, and design
First Folio Resource Group, Inc.
    Erinn Banting
    Tom Dart
    Söğüt Y. Güleç
    Alana Lai
    Debbie Smith

Editing
Carolyn Black

Separations and film
Embassy Graphics

Printer
Worzalla Publishing Company

Consultants
Elisa de Carranza, Consulate General of El Salvador, Houston; Ana Cecilia Romero and Patricia Zepeda, Consulate of El Salvador, Toronto

Photographs
Martin Adler/Panos Pictures: p. 6; AP/Wide World Photos: p. 10 (both); Allan Barnes/DDB Stock Photo: p. 16 (bottom); Wesley Bocxe/Photo Researchers: p. 23; Jules Bucher/Photo Researchers: p. 9; J. P. Courau/DDB Stock Photo: p. 18 (bottom), p. 21 (bottom), p. 24; Gregory G. Dimijian: p. 31 (bottom); Lizzette Marenco de Dreyfus: p. 19 (right); Michael Everett/DDB Stock Photo: p. 5, p. 17 (left); Robert Francis/Hutchison Library: title page, p. 19 (left); Greg Johnston: cover, p. 7 (both), p. 8 (both), p. 14 (top), p. 15

(bottom), p. 18 (top), p. 22, p. 25 (bottom), p. 27 (top), p. 28, p. 29 (both), p. 30; Alison M. Jones: p. 12 (top), p. 15 (top), p. 21 (top); Tom McHugh/Photo Researchers: p. 31 (top); John Mitchell: p. 14 (bottom), p. 20 (bottom); Richard Powers/Life File: p. 4 (top), p. 16 (top), p. 27 (bottom); Reuters/Kimberly White/Archive Photos: p. 11; Chris R. Sharp/DDB Stock Photo: p. 25 (top); Sean Sprague/Panos Pictures: p. 4 (bottom), p. 17 (right), p. 20 (top), p. 26; Anneke van Gijzen: p. 3, p. 13; Eric Velado: p. 12 (bottom)

Map
Jim Chernishenko

Illustrations
Dianne Eastman: icon
David Wysotski, Allure Illustrations: back cover

Cover: A man collects water from a river that rushes through the dense forest in the Montecristo Mountains. Some trees in the forest, such as oaks and laurels, grow to more than 98 feet (30 meters) tall.

Title page: Two men row their fishing boats through the swampy Lake El Jocotal near San Miguel, in eastern El Salvador. The lake and its surrounding areas make up the El Jocotal Wildlife Refuge, where endangered species, such as the white heron, are protected.

Icon: A coffee plant's berries, which are harvested, dried, and roasted to make coffee beans, appear at the head of each section.

Back cover: The *tigrillo*, or ocelot, is a small wildcat that lives in the mountainous regions of El Salvador.

Published by
Crabtree Publishing Company

PMB 16A,
350 Fifth Avenue
Suite 3308
New York
N.Y. 10118

612 Welland Avenue
St. Catharines
Ontario, Canada
L2M 5V6

73 Lime Walk
Headington
Oxford OX3 7AD
United Kingdom

Cataloging in Publication Data

Nickles, Greg, 1969-
    El Salvador. The land / Greg Nickles
        p. cm. -- (The lands, peoples and cultures series)
        Includes index.
    Summary: Describes the geography, climate, people, cities, farming, industry, and changing economy of El Salvador.
        ISBN 0-7787-9367-2 (RLB) -- ISBN 0-7787-9735-X (pbk.)
    1. El Salvador--Description and travel--Juvenile literature. [1. El Salvador.] I. Series.
F1484.3 .N53 2002
972.84--dc21
                                                    2001032529
                                                    LC

Contents

 # Lush and beautiful

El Salvador is a warm, lush, and beautiful country. It lies along the Pacific shore of the **isthmus** that joins North and South America. The smallest of the seven countries that make up Central America, it is only about 150 miles (240 kilometers) from east to west and 50 miles (80 kilometers) from north to south. In spite of its small size, El Salvador has many different landforms. There are volcanic mountains, lakes in **craters**, broad plains, sandy beaches, and hundreds of rivers.

Developing nation

El Salvador is sometimes called a "developing nation." This means that its industries are changing from those based mainly on farming and **natural resources** to those based on manufacturing and services, such as banking or communications. Many of the changes in El Salvador took place after the **civil war**, which lasted from 1979 until 1992. Rebuilding from the war's destruction, as well as from devastating earthquakes and hurricanes, is a continuing challenge for Salvadorans.

(above) Two boys load lemongrass, a sweet grass used to season food, onto a cart near Usulután, a city in southern El Salvador.

(top) Three children play beneath a waterfall at Los Chorros, a natural gorge near San Salvador.

(opposite) Lake Ilopango, a crater lake, was created inside a volcano when the top of the volcano collapsed.

4

Facts at a glance

Official name: *República de El Salvador*
 (Republic of El Salvador)
Area: 8,124 square miles
 (21,040 square kilometers)
Population: 6,122,515
Capital: San Salvador
Main language: Spanish
Main religion: Roman Catholicism
Currency: *colon*
National holiday: Independence Day,
 September 15 (1821)

Between mountains and the sea

Low shrubs, grass, and trees grow in the Chalatenango region, in northern El Salvador.

Gigantic mountains tower over El Salvador's landscape. Some of these mountains are active volcanoes, with clouds of ash and smoke spewing into the sky. In the shadow of the mountains, there are farms, rivers, lakes, small woodlands, and bustling cities and towns.

Northern mountains

The north and northeast parts of El Salvador are very rugged. Two large mountain chains, the Metapán and Chalatenango, rise along the northern border. They range in height from 5,000 to 6,500 feet (1,500 to 1,900 meters). Some of the mountains are made of limestone, which is a soft rock, but most are made of basalt, a dark rock formed from the lava and ash of volcanoes. Narrow, green valleys with fast-moving streams lie between the mountain peaks. The streams are fed by rainwater that runs off the mountains. Very few Salvadorans live on farms and in villages scattered throughout this rough landscape.

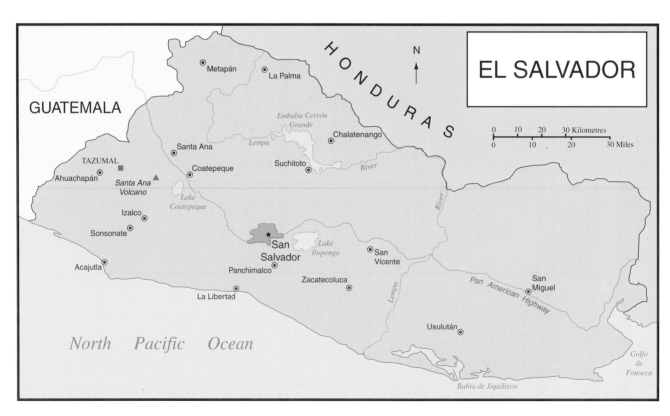

*(above) The Lempa River is over 200 miles
(320 kilometers) long.*

Central plains

Below the northern mountains, toward the center of the country, lies a narrow area of flat, **fertile** plains. Farmers plant crops and raise **livestock** in this region. El Salvador's major river, the Lempa, winds through the plains, collecting water from mountain streams on its way to the Pacific coast.

Southern volcanoes

South of the plains, running west to east in two rows, stand more than 20 major volcanoes. Only a few of these volcanoes are active. Fiery lava underneath the volcanoes heats water that spurts to the earth's surface, and creates hot springs and boiling patches of mud called mudpots.

Deep, bright blue lakes sit in several volcanic craters, or calderas. Lakes Coatepeque and Ilopango are two of El Salvador's largest crater lakes.

*(left) A small waterfall in the northern
mountains rushes over a rocky basalt cliff into
a shallow pool below.*

Santa Ana and Izalco

The Santa Ana volcano is one of El Salvador's tallest peaks, at 7,812 feet (2,381 meters). After its most recent eruption in 1920, a small lake formed in its crater. The lake's **sulfurous** water, produced by volcanoes, smells like rotten eggs.

El Salvador's most famous volcano is Izalco, which is nicknamed *"El Faro del Pacífico"* or "Lighthouse of the Pacific." Salvadorans say that this black, barren mountain was once just a hole in the ground. Beginning in 1770, the hole spewed smoke and glowing-hot lava almost continuously until the 1960s, building the volcano into the mountain it is today. Izalco glowed so brightly that sailors used it as a lighthouse to guide their ships at night.

(left) The Izalco volcano, in western El Salvador, has erupted more than 51 times since 1770.

(below) Fields and trees cover the rolling hills of the central highlands.

A beach covered in black sand sits amid trees and rocky cliffs on the Pacific coast.

The central highlands

Rolling highlands sit between El Salvador's southern mountains. Despite danger from the surrounding volcanoes, this region is the country's most densely populated area. As many as 75 percent of Salvadorans live here, mostly in major cities such as the **capital**, San Salvador. Dark, fertile soil, formed from volcanic ash and rock, attracted settlers to the highlands. Farmland, mostly used to grow coffee, surrounds the region's many villages and cities.

The Pacific coast

Mighty ocean waves pound El Salvador's Pacific coast. The coastline is made up of a narrow strip of beaches, rocky cliffs, and lowlands. Black sand, formed from the region's dark volcanic rock, covers the beaches. Resort towns along the coast are a favorite vacation spot for Salvadorans, who love to relax in the sun, swim, or watch the water for an occasional dolphin or sea turtle.

Bays and gulfs

On the east side of El Salvador is a bay, called the Bahía de Jiquilisco, and a gulf, named Golfo de Fonseca. Both bodies of water shelter many islands, including Conchagüita. According to legend, pirates took over Conchagüita in 1682 and used it as their secret base. Later, it became deserted, but Salvadorans resettled it in the 1920s. Ruins of the pirates' settlement can still be seen today.

Many rivers

For such a small country, El Salvador has many rivers. More than 300 flow through the land, almost all draining into the Pacific Ocean. Their water comes from rain, which falls on the mountains and then trickles down the slopes. The water often looks muddy because of the soil it carries with it down the mountainsides. Most rivers are shallow and filled with **silt**, or blocked by plants, rocks, and other obstacles. Of all the rivers in the country, only part of the Lempa has areas clear enough for boats to pass through.

Weather and natural hazards

El Salvador's climate is tropical, which means that it is hot and often humid, or damp, year-round. Temperatures range between 75°F and 95°F (24°C and 34°C). Sudden downpours and exhausting heat are a part of daily life. Only in the high mountains is the weather cooler. Occasionally, hurricanes or other natural disasters, such as volcanic eruptions and earthquakes, disturb the landscape.

El Salvador is close to the equator, a part of the earth that receives almost the same amount of sunlight at every time of year. El Salvador has about twelve hours of sunlight each day. The sun always rises between 5:00 and 5:30 in the morning and sets between 5:30 and 6:00 in the evening.

(above) **People wade through knee-deep water after a temporale. Temporales** *are heavy downpours that last for five to eight consecutive days.*

Humid weather

El Salvador is often very humid. Warm winds from the Pacific Ocean carry moisture through the air. As these winds pass over El Salvador, the moisture falls as rain. El Salvador's mountain slopes receive more rain than anywhere else in the country — more than 80 inches (200 centimeters) each year.

(left) **A boy pours a bowl of water on his head to cool down on a hot day in San Salvador.**

Wet and dry seasons

It usually rains every day during *invierno*, the wet season that runs from May to October. Huge, black clouds gather during the afternoon, bringing storms with spectacular lightning by evening. Less rain falls during *verano*, the dry season between November and April.

Warm winds and hurricanes

Extreme weather occasionally threatens El Salvador. The late 1990s were especially difficult for the country because of both droughts, long periods of time when no rain falls, and floods. El Niño, a pocket of unusually warm weather over the Pacific Ocean, caused droughts beginning in 1997. Then, in 1998, a huge Atlantic storm called Hurricane Mitch battered El Salvador with gusting winds and rain. The hurricane caused large floods and landslides throughout the east, sweeping away crops, livestock, roads, and homes. More than 200 Salvadorans died from Hurricane Mitch.

Eruptions and earthquakes

El Salvador, sometimes called the "Land of Volcanoes," has frequent eruptions and earthquakes. There have been eleven eruptions in the last 50 years. Scientists believe that these eruptions and earthquakes are caused by moving layers of rock, called tectonic plates, far under the earth's surface. El Salvador sits on the edges of three tectonic plates. As the plates shift, they scrape against one another. The scraping is so powerful that it causes tremors, creates heat, and releases poisonous gases underground. Eruptions happen when pressure builds up so much that gases and lava explode from the earth's surface.

On January 13, 2001, El Salvador was struck by an earthquake measuring 7.6 on the Richter scale. A month later, a second earthquake, measuring 6.6 on the Richter scale, hit El Salvador. By February 20, 1,127 people were dead, 7,660 were injured, 310,000 homes were destroyed, and more than 1.5 million people were left homeless.

The Salvadorans

Most Salvadorans are of mixed **ancestry**. They are the **descendants** of Spanish settlers who intermarried with El Salvador's Native peoples hundreds of years ago. Only a few groups of Native peoples who did not intermarry with the Spanish still live in El Salvador today. Another small group of Salvadorans is made up of people solely of European or other ancestry.

Native peoples past and present

Native peoples have lived in El Salvador for thousands of years. They developed complex **cultures**, with their own languages, traditions, sciences, and cities. These Native peoples were the region's only inhabitants until about 500 years ago, when European **conquerors** first came from Spain. Through war, disease, and slavery, Spanish rulers eventually killed most of the Native peoples. Those who survived suffered horribly under their country's governments through the 1800s and 1900s.

People estimate that about 60,000 Native people live in El Salvador today. Physically, they look similar to other Salvadorans, and many speak Spanish and follow Spanish customs. As a result, it is difficult to tell Native people apart from other Salvadorans. The Pipíl are the largest known group of Native peoples in El Salvador. They live mostly in villages in the southwest, where they preserve some of their traditional culture.

(left) This woman lives in Acajulta, a port in southwestern El Salvador.

(below) Three generations pose for a family picture at a reunion in Izalco, in western El Salvador.

These children are learning to carry water jugs on their heads. When they are older, they will use the jugs to bring water from nearby rivers to their homes.

Native and European

Salvadorans of mixed Native and Spanish ancestry make up over 90 percent of the country's population. Their European ancestors came from Spain beginning in the 1500s, searching for riches and land for their king. Spanish men who settled in El Salvador married and had children with Native women. Today, the descendants of mixed Native and Spanish parents speak Spanish.

Other Salvadorans

As many as five percent of Salvadorans are the direct descendants of the wealthy Spanish rulers who controlled El Salvador from the 1500s until the 1800s. Many of their families remain rich and powerful today. They hold important positions in the government and military, and they own most Salvadoran property and big businesses.

El Salvador is also home to thousands of people of Lebanese, Palestinian, and Jewish background whose ancestors **immigrated** in the 1800s. In the last 100 years, Americans, Japanese, and people of other nationalities have moved to the country, usually to set up businesses.

Rich and poor

One of the largest factors that separates Salvadorans from one another is money. A small number of people have almost all the country's wealth. There is a growing middle class, with people who live fairly comfortably. Many Salvadorans, however, do not have enough money to house, feed, and clothe their families. Over the years, this unfair situation led to violence in the country, including the civil war, which claimed the lives of more than 75,000 Salvadorans.

Salvadorans abroad

Today, hundreds of thousands of people who are originally from El Salvador live in countries surrounding El Salvador and in North America. More than one million Salvadorans fled to these places during the civil war. Many **refugees** found jobs and homes in their new countries. Once the war was over, some returned to El Salvador, but others decided to stay where they were. They began to build new lives and send some of the money they earned to relatives still in El Salvador.

Traces of the Maya

El Salvador once belonged to the great Mayan **empire**. The Maya developed advanced systems of **architecture**, mathematics, **astronomy**, and agriculture. They also invented a complex system of writing, and created beautiful sculptures and carvings. Today, millions of Mayan descendants live throughout Central America, including the Lenca people of El Salvador.

An empire in ruins

El Salvador lay in the southernmost part of the Mayan empire. By 1200 B.C., the Maya had built towns and cities there. These included their capital, Tazumal, in the west and San Andrés, to its east. After thriving for hundreds of years, the empire crumbled around 900 A.D. The Maya abandoned their cities, which became overgrown with jungle. No one knows exactly what brought an end to the Mayan empire. Some people think that a series of famines, or widespread food shortages, and wars is to blame.

(right) This stone carving, found at the ruins of Tazumal, is over 2,000 years old.

(top) Mayan nobles were buried in the massive step pyramid in San Andrés.

Cities once strong

The ruins of ancient Mayan statues and buildings show how advanced the Maya were in the arts and sciences. They constructed step-pyramid temples from expertly cut stone blocks. They pulled, pushed, and carried these blocks to each site without the use of wheels or animals. At Tazumal and San Andrés, **archaeologists** found ruins of tombs, sports fields, and marketplaces, as well as pottery, jewelry, and other **artifacts**.

Joya de Cerén

A lot of what we know about the Maya was discovered in El Salvador, at a site called Joya de Cerén, or "Jewel of Cerén." About 1,400 years ago, it was a thriving Mayan farming village. Then, the nearby Laguna Caldera volcano exploded and the Maya abandoned the village. For centuries, 20 feet (6 meters) of ash and lava buried Joya de Cerén. The village was rediscovered in 1976.

Unearthing the past

Excavation of Joya de Cerén uncovered well-preserved houses and other stone buildings, everyday tools, pottery, and jars of seeds. From these seeds, archaeologists could tell that the Mayan farmers grew and ate chiles, corn, squash, beans, and cacao. These and other discoveries were so important that the United Nations Educational, Scientific, and Cultural Organization (UNESCO) declared Joya de Cerén a protected World Heritage Site in 1993.

(above) A Mayan farmer dances at a harvest festival in this painting, which was discovered on a wall at the ruins of Joya de Cerén.

(below) Archaeologists at San Andrés use small brushes, tiny picks, and other special tools to carefully clean the dirt off ancient Mayan artifacts and ruins.

San Salvador and other cities

Most Salvadoran cities grew from small Spanish settlements founded hundreds of years ago. Today, they are home to the majority of El Salvador's people and industries. Some cities have many beautiful, old buildings. Others look much newer because their historic buildings were destroyed by natural disasters and wars, or torn down to build new homes, businesses, factories, and roads. All Salvadoran cities have outdoor markets; *comedores*, or cafés; and *pupuserias*. *Pupuserias* are street stalls and restaurants that sell *pupusas*, fat tortillas stuffed with cheese, pork, or beans.

(right) Intricate carvings decorate the outside of the Basílica del Sagrado Corazón, in San Salvador. Built during the 1900s, the church is one of the few buildings that was not destroyed during San Salvador's many earthquakes.

(below) San Salvador's outdoor markets are filled with fresh fruit and vegetables, canned goods, and household supplies.

San Salvador's history

San Salvador is El Salvador's capital. With about one-quarter of the country's population, San Salvador is also the largest city in El Salvador. The Pipíl were the first known inhabitants of this area. They were conquered in 1525 by the Spanish, who built their own settlement nearby. The Spaniards named the settlement in honor of Jesus Christ, who Christians believe is the son of God. Christ is sometimes called the "Holy Savior," which in Spanish is *"San Salvador."*

As San Salvador grew over the centuries, its residents built churches, monuments, government buildings, and grand *plazas* or squares. Unfortunately, only a handful of the beautiful buildings constructed more than 100 years ago still stand. Almost all were destroyed by earthquakes and flooding.

(above) *The Democracy Building, in downtown San Salvador, was damaged by an earthquake in 1996. The high-rise has since been repaired.*

The streets of San Salvador

Cars, buses, and trucks jam the streets of downtown San Salvador. The government has built dozens of bridges and highways to help thin out these traffic jams. On the sidewalks, thousands of pedestrians weave their way between vendors. Acrobats or *mariachi* bands occasionally perform on street corners. Cranes and **scaffolding** rise between shopping malls, churches, restaurants, theaters, and apartments.

San Salvador's suburbs are not as hectic as downtown. Those to the west of the city have mostly comfortable houses and apartments, surrounded by stylish shops, theaters, and restaurants. The suburbs to the east have *colonias*, which are neighborhoods with thousands of small houses built with bricks and cement, and areas with one-room homes made of concrete blocks, scrap wood, tin, and mud.

(above) *Many Salvadorans whose homes were destroyed during the civil war or after earthquakes and hurricanes live in one-room houses made from tin and brick on the outskirts of San Salvador.*

Santa Ana

Santa Ana sits on the northeast slope of the Santa Ana volcano, which is sometimes called "father hill." It is the second largest city in El Salvador. Even though it was damaged during the civil war, it still has many beautiful buildings dating from the years of Spanish rule. Two of the most famous are the El Calvario church and Santa Ana's cathedral. Inside the cathedral, archways soar high over artwork that is hundreds of years old.

Santa Ana became one of the country's most important cities partly because it is a large center for producing sugar cane and coffee. Grown in the fields around Santa Ana, coffee beans are sent to El Molino, one of Santa Ana's huge coffee mills, and then packed to be shipped overseas.

(above) The city of Suchitoto, in central El Salvador, gets its name from the Native Nahuatl language, and means "Place of Bird and Flower."

(below) The Teatro Santa Ana was built in the 1930s. Musical and theatrical performances still take place in the theater today.

Shops and restaurants crowd a main street in San Miguel.

San Vicente

The city of San Vicente, in central El Salvador, sits beneath a huge, twin-peaked volcano named Chinchontepec. San Vicente was founded in 1635 for people solely of Spanish descent. At that time, **racist** laws prohibited Spanish and Native peoples from living together. Today, most residents of San Vicente are of mixed ancestry. The city's famous landmarks include the Torre Kiosko, an unusual white clock tower that stands in the city's central park; the Iglesia el Pilar, one of the country's oldest churches; and a busy outdoor market that spans many streets.

San Vicente is known for a rebellion that began nearby in 1833. During the uprising, Salvadoran hero Anastasio Aquino, who fought for the Native peoples against the Spanish, took over San Vicente. Two months later, the Spanish recaptured the city. Aquino lost the rebellion, but the people of San Vicente never forgot his bravery.

San Miguel

San Miguel, in eastern El Salvador, sits on the slopes of two volcanoes. Eruptions are common in this city. One volcano, named Chaparrastique, is especially active. It has erupted about ten times in the last 100 years. Like other places in El Salvador, San Miguel has had to rebuild itself after these eruptions.

Early in San Miguel's history, **prospectors** discovered gold nearby and became wealthy. Later, people made money from the sale and trade of crops such as sugar cane, coffee, and grain, which grew in fields surrounding the city. San Miguel became known as the "Pearl of the East" because of its wealth and hard-working people.

From the top of the Torre Kiosko, people can see the entire city of San Vicente. Since the clock tower was damaged during the recent earthquake, people have not been able to climb to its top.

Farming and fishing

El Salvador's economy was built on agriculture. For hundreds of years, farmers have grown crops and raised livestock. More recently, fishing has become an important source of income for the country.

The fishing industry

Salvadorans catch shark, lobster, anchovies, shrimp, snapper, and grouper in the Pacific Ocean. Although people have fished in the Pacific Ocean for many years, the government only recently began to encourage fishing as an industry. Government-run projects instruct and help fishers in small fishing companies and in cooperatives. Cooperatives are owned by all the workers, who share decisions and profits equally.

(left) The fishers of La Libertad, in southern El Salvador, sell their catch at an outdoor market.

(top) People harvest maize, or corn, at a farm near Chalatenango, in the north. Maize is a main part of the Salvadoran diet.

Crops and livestock

Salvadoran farmers grow a wide variety of tropical fruits along the Pacific coast. These include cantaloupes, watermelons, avocados, bananas, oranges, mangoes, and coconuts. Rice, beans, and corn, which are a main part of the Salvadoran diet, grow throughout the country. Farmers also raise livestock — mainly chickens, cattle, and pigs — wherever the soil is not good for growing crops.

Sold worldwide

Most of El Salvador's rich farmland produces crops that are sold around the world. These crops include sugar cane, oilseed, and coffee. Cotton, grown along the Pacific coast, was once an important crop, but the civil war forced farmers to abandon their **plantations**. Recently, some farmers have started raising tropical flowers and seeds, such as poppy and sesame, for **export** to other countries.

(above) Cattle wait to be fed on a farm in La Paz, a region in the south.

(below) Once sugar cane is harvested, it is loaded onto trucks and taken to a refinery where it is made into refined sugar.

Coffee plantations

Throughout El Salvador, fields of coffee plants surround towns and cities. The country's coffee industry is one of the largest in the world. The first coffee plantations were established by wealthy Salvadorans over 140 years ago. They realized that the rich volcanic mountain soil and tropical climate were ideal for growing coffee plants. Coffee soon replaced indigo, a plant used to make a rich blue dye, as the land's major crop.

El Salvador's wealthiest families still control the country's coffee trade. They live in luxurious mansions and hire local farmers to plant and harvest their crops. Recently, the Salvadoran government began converting large coffee plantations into thousands of small cooperatives.

Coffee plants grow in long rows on a plantation in the northern mountains.

Tending the beans

Coffee is made from beans that grow inside the berries of the coffee plant. Salvadorans raise a type of coffee plant called arabica, which grows very well on the slopes of El Salvador's volcanic mountains. Growing coffee plants is a difficult process that must be done by hand. Only an experienced worker can tell which berries are ripe and should be picked, and which should remain on the plant. To add to the challenge, the slopes on which coffee plants grow are sometimes so steep that farmers use ropes to scale them for pruning or harvesting.

The picking season for coffee beans lasts from November to January, at the same time that children are on vacation from school. Many Salvadoran children who live on farms work on coffee plantations during the picking season. Some children earn money to buy school supplies, clothing, and Christmas presents for their families.

After being picked, coffee beans are left to dry in the sun. Then, they are shoveled into piles and put into bags so they can be transported to other parts of El Salvador and the world.

Hulled, dried, and bagged

After the harvest, the coffee beans are removed from the berries and then **hulled** and dried. Most beans are packed in sacks for export. The beans are shipped unroasted because roasted beans immediately begin to lose their flavor. Instead, they are roasted just before buyers sell them to customers.

Roasting for flavor

Only experts can roast coffee beans to bring out their finest flavor. They place the beans in large ovens that must be carefully timed. Just a minute's extra roasting can ruin an entire batch! The beans pop and hiss in the heat as they turn to a rich brown color. After seven minutes, they may be removed to make light roast coffee, which has a mild flavor. Beans roasted for nine to eleven minutes are called medium roast, and those left in for twelve to thirteen minutes are called dark roast. The richest flavor is called espresso. It comes from beans roasted fourteen minutes, until they are black. Espresso coffee has a very strong, burnt flavor.

El Salvador's public·works programs, which are funded by the government, help cities build more modern sewage systems and new homes.

For many years, Salvadorans have worked hard to improve their lives. They have been repairing the damage from the civil war and from natural disasters, and encouraging local people and foreign companies to open new businesses.

Money from afar

Over the last 20 years, other countries have lent El Salvador money to help develop its industries and **infrastructure**. After the civil war, more foreign companies also began to invest in businesses there. Most money from afar is sent by Salvadorans who live and work in other countries, to help relatives in their homeland. Foreign support, combined with local Salvadoran ideas and hard work, has slowly improved the standard of living for many.

Manufacturing

Today, El Salvador's manufacturing industry is growing. Plants **refine** petroleum and chemicals, or make building materials such as light metals and cement. Factories produce electronics and textiles, two of the country's strongest industries.

Powering the nation

Salvadorans use their country's abundant sources of natural energy to power their factories and homes. Dams cross parts of the Lempa River to create **hydroelectricity**, the most important source of electricity in the country. Fuel, such as petroleum, comes from Venezuela and the United States.

Environmental problems

El Salvador's developing industries cause serious environmental problems. Erosion on mountain slopes, caused by the cutting of trees, washes away fertile soil and clogs hydroelectric dams with mud. Many rivers contain poisons dumped by industries. **Exhaust** from vehicles and factories chokes cities. This pollution is responsible for breathing problems and diseases that harm both people and wildlife.

Hot stuff

The most promising source of energy in El Salvador is underground. Salvadorans are experimenting with geothermal power, which is created by volcanic heat. The best-known geothermal site is near the city of Ahuachapán, in western El Salvador. It is called Los Ausoles or "The Cauldrons." Los Ausoles earned its name from the boiling mudpots, **geysers**, hot springs, and bright red, steaming earth that can be found there.

To tap the earth's thermal energy, workers at Los Ausoles pump water through wells that are drilled over half a mile (one kilometer) into the hot ground. As the water heats up, some of it changes into steam. The steam spins powerful **turbines** that create electricity.

Attracting tourists

Before the civil war ended in 1992, tourists did not visit El Salvador. Even Salvadorans rarely traveled within their own country, except to the beaches. Today, many Salvadorans travel regularly to the countryside on Sundays and holidays. The government is also trying to attract visitors from other countries by helping foreign companies build new hotels in El Salvador.

(above) A worker inspects one of the wells at a geothermal power plant.

(below) White-water rafting through the rough waters of the Lempa River is a favorite tourist activity.

Getting around

How you get around in El Salvador depends on where you are. People in cities walk, bicycle, ride buses, take a taxi, or drive to get from place to place.

Traveling in the countryside is more difficult than traveling in the city because the roads are mostly unpaved. Instead, they are packed with dirt and gravel. During the rainy season, they can become difficult to travel on, especially in the mountains where mudslides are a constant danger. People in the countryside usually walk or bicycle, although some ride horses or mules. To get to a neighboring town, they usually take a very bumpy bus ride.

Pile in!

When passengers board a bus, they toss their luggage into the back or on a rack on the roof. Often, the driver's helper, who is usually a young boy, assists them. Inside, the buses can get hot and crowded. Passengers squeeze three to a seat. Anyone who cannot find a seat must stand, sometimes for the entire trip. Along the way, the bus stops frequently to pick up new passengers. If very bad weather hits, the driver may stop on the roadside for hours, waiting for driving conditions to improve.

A farmer and his son use a cart pulled by two bulls to transport goods to the market.

(above) Most Salvadoran buses are sturdy school buses that the drivers decorate themselves.

City traffic

Drivers in the city move very slowly. The traffic has become heavier there because more and more people own cars. Some of these cars are gifts from relatives who live in the United States. The relatives buy old cars and drive them to El Salvador to give to their families. Streets are also jammed with pedestrians, performers singing to drivers for money, and street vendors who tap on car windows, hoping to sell their goods.

(right) Shoppers on their way home from the market hitch a ride on the back of a pickup truck. They have to be careful to hold on tightly so they do not fall off!

Plants and wildlife

El Salvador's small forests are home to a variety of interesting plants and animals. Unfortunately, much of the landscape has been cleared for farmland or ruined by pollution, destroying many plant and animal **habitats.** Today, environmentalists work hard to preserve what remains of El Salvador's wildlife.

Patches of forest

Only small patches of forest remain in El Salvador. Oak and pine trees grow on mountain slopes; mangrove trees flourish in swampy areas; and palm and coconut trees grow along the coast.

(top) Crocodiles mainly live in El Salvador's freshwater rivers or lakes, where they can feed on fish, insects, and small animals that live near the water.

Bálsamo trees

Some of El Salvador's most beautiful trees are *bálsamo*, or balsa, trees. They are found by the seaside and in rainforests. These trees grow very quickly. In just ten years, they can reach up to 90 feet (27 meters). Their height and broad leaves help shield plants from the scorching sun. People use the *bálsamo* tree's extremely tough, but light, wood to build models, boats, and aircraft. They also use the tree's resin or sap, which is called balsam, in perfumes and traditional medicines. Workers collect the balsam in rags, which they stuff into holes cut in the trunks of *bálsamo* trees. To help the balsam flow, they sometimes heat the trunk with small, burning pieces of wood. Once the rags soak up enough resin, the workers remove and boil them to release the balsam.

Toucans are well known for their brightly colored beaks and faces.

Astonishing orchids

More than 200 varieties of orchids grow in El Salvador's rainforests. They thrive on plants that rot in the tropical heat and humidity. Although orchids often look quite different from one another, most blossoms have one distinctly shaped and colored petal, called the lip, which hangs lower than the rest. Each flower produces more than two million seeds!

Toucans are well known for their brightly colored beaks and faces.

Beautiful white and purple orchids grow in the Montecristo Cloud Forest.

The Montecristo Cloud Forest

High on the Montecristo mountain, in northwestern El Salvador, stands a beautiful **nature reserve** called El Trifinio. El Trifinio is shared and protected by El Salvador, Guatemala, and Honduras. It contains the remarkable Montecristo Cloud Forest. A cloud forest is a type of rainforest that is found in mountains and is always covered in a thick, cloudlike mist. The trees and plants grow so close together that raindrops from the frequent showers overhead never make it to the ground. Instead, they splatter against the leaves. The thick moisture in the air and the forest's cool temperature combine to form the mist.

Lichens and mosses grow everywhere in the Montecristo Cloud Forest, especially on the trunks of the enormous pine, oak, and cypress trees. Toucans fly among the trees, and monkeys swing from branch to branch. Among the giant ferns, orchids, and other plants on the forest floor, wander animals such as wild pigs, anteaters, and sometimes jaguars.

(above) **The tigrillo** *lives mainly on the ground, but is also a nimble tree climber.*

(opposite) A thick mist covers the plants, flowers, and ancient trees that grow in the Montecristo Cloud Forest.

(below) A male quetzal's tail feathers can grow to be 24 inches (61 centimeters) long, which is nearly twice the length of its body!

Protecting nature

In addition to El Trifinio, the Cerro Verde National Park and the Bosque el Imposible National Park protect parts of the country's remaining mountain habitats. The lush Cerro Verde perches on the Cerro Verde mountain, an extinct volcano in the west. The remote Bosque el Imposible, in southwest El Salvador, got its name because it is nearly impossible to reach. Among the hundreds of plant and animal species that live there is the *tigrillo*, or ocelot. This small wildcat can be identified by the rows of large dark brown or black spots on its back and its whitish belly. The *tigrillo* is most active at night, when it hunts for birds, insects, and frogs.

In the air

Beautiful butterflies of all colors, shapes, and sizes flutter throughout El Salvador. Also in the sky are many different types of birds, such as wild ducks, blue jays, and herons. The most famous bird in El Salvador is the rare quetzal, found on the Montecristo mountain. A quetzal's back glitters blue. Its very long tail is blue-green on top and white underneath. On its head is a crest that looks like fuzzy hair. The ancient Mayan people considered the quetzal sacred. They wove its feathers, which they thought more valuable than gold, into ceremonial clothing and headdresses. According to legend, the quetzal's belly was stained crimson red with the blood of a Mayan leader killed by Spanish invaders.

Glossary

ancestry The people from whom one is descended

archaeologist A person who studies the past by looking at buildings and artifacts

architecture The science and art of designing and constructing buildings

artifact A product, usually historical, made by human craft

astronomy The study of the stars and planets

capital A city where the government of a state or country is located

civil war A war between different groups of people within a country

conqueror A person who gains control of land or a group of people using force

crater A pit at the mouth of a volcano

culture The customs, beliefs, and arts of a distinct group of people

descendant A person who can trace his or her family roots to a certain family or group

empire A group of countries or territories with the same ruler or government

excavation The act of digging up

exhaust The fumes or gas released from a car or another machine

export To sell to another country

fertile Able to produce abundant crops or vegetation

geyser A hot stream that shoots water and steam into the air

habitat The area or environment in which plants or animals are normally found

hulled To have the outer covering of a fruit, seed, or nut removed

hydroelectricity Electricity produced by the flow of water

immigrate To settle in a different country

infrastructure The basic services and facilities that a community or society needs

isthmus A strip of land that connects two larger areas

livestock Farm animals

natural resource A material found in nature, such as oil, coal, minerals, or timber

nature reserve A park where nature is protected

plantation A large farm on which crops, such as cotton, coffee, and sugar, are grown

prospector A person who explores an area for minerals or precious metals

racist Treating a group of people unfairly based on their ethnic background

refine To purify

refugee A person who leaves his or her home or country because of danger

scaffolding A raised platform that holds workers repairing a building

silt A sand-like material

sulfurous Mixed with a chemical called sulfur

turbine An engine that uses water, steam, or air to make it move

 # Index